THE TWENTY-FIRST CENTURY MOSES

Blessed Bernard C. Rauckhorst
Per John, Chapter 20, verse 29

outskirtspress
DENVER, COLORADO

The opinions expressed in this manuscript are solely the opinions of the author and do not represent the opinions or thoughts of the publisher. The author has represented and warranted full ownership and/or legal right to publish all the materials in this book.

The Twenty-First Century Moses
All Rights Reserved.
Copyright © 2015 Bernard C. Rauckhorst
v2.0

Cover Photo © 2015 Laura McDowell. All rights reserved - used with permission.

This book may not be reproduced, transmitted, or stored in whole or in part by any means, including graphic, electronic, or mechanical without the express written consent of the publisher except in the case of brief quotations embodied in critical articles and reviews.

Outskirts Press, Inc.
http://www.outskirtspress.com

ISBN: 978-1-4787-4301-9

Outskirts Press and the "OP" logo are trademarks belonging to Outskirts Press, Inc.

PRINTED IN THE UNITED STATES OF AMERICA

This book is dedicated to the following people:
        Albert and Rose Rauckhorst (my great parents)
        Andrew and Mary Fuerst (my outstanding in-laws)
        And Alice Rauckhorst (my wonderful wife)
This dedication makes this a five "Star" document.

Acknowledgements

Our Heavenly Father is the prime reason for this book, followed by the Holy Spirit with Jesus and Mary. Several of the Saints like Joseph, the spouse of Mary, and John the apostle sending guidance to me through my wonderful wife Alice.

My daughter, Laura McDowell, who took the task of editing the book for spelling and sentence structure and then putting it on the Internet, was indispensable.

Many thanks to my son-in-law, Glenn McDowell, for putting the front cover together per my desire.

Table of Contents

1. The Sin of the Vatican 1
2. Background 3
3. The People 6
4. Slavery 8
5. Moses: First and Second 9
6. Intimacy With God 12
7. The End of Slavery for the Israelites 14
8. The New Moses Plan in General 17
9. The Devil Problems 21
10. Incomprehensible Behavior 24
11. The Tribes of the Israelites 25
12. Weekly Worship 27
13. The Boring Mass 29
14. Abortion 31
15. Mary the Refuge of Sinners 32
16. The Rosary 34
17. The Bronze Serpent 37
18. Our Nation – America [Nineveh] 39
19. The Prizes – Canaan / Heaven 41

20. Our Leader's Requirements 43
21. The Bottom Line 45
22. A Misunderstanding of Mary's Power 47
23. A Note to the Generals 48

Appendix I: The Prayer of Abandonment to God 51
Appendix II: Appointed Generals and Their Locations 52
Appendix III: Devotion to Mary 55
Appendix IV: Consecration to Mary Immaculate 58
Appendix V: Prayers of the Rosary 59
Appendix VI: Prayer to Our Lady of the Miraculous Medal 62
Biblical Reference 63
Contact the Author 64

1

The Sin of the Vatican

In 1917, Our Lady appeared at Fatima and requested the Consecration of Russia to Her Immaculate Heart and on the first Saturdays of each month, Communion for Reparation of sins.

In 1929, Our Lady appeared to Lucia (of Fatima fame) at Tuy and asked for the fulfillment of Her previous request. "I shall come to ask for the Consecration of Russia to My Immaculate Heart… If they heed My request, <u>Russia will be converted and there will be peace</u>." Our Lady explained that this consecration should be made by the Holy Father in union with all of the Bishops of the world.

The Virgin Mary appeared in May of 1952 to Lucia of Fatima and said: "<u>Make it known to the Holy Father that I am always awaiting the Consecration of Russia to My Immaculate Heart. Without that Consecration, Russia will not be able to convert, nor will the world have peace.</u>"

The fourth commandment of the Decalog (The Ten Commandments) is: "Honor your father and mother." Here we have the Mother of God, our Spiritual Mother, the Mother of the Church making a request and the Catholic Hierarchy not paying heed.

It reminds me of the story of Naaman, the commander of the King of Aram's army, who sought help from the Jewish prophet Elisha to be cured of leprosy. Elisha sent a message to him saying, "Go wash in the Jordan River seven times and your flesh will be restored." Naaman became angry. He went away saying, "I thought that for me he would surely come out, and stand and call on the name of the Lord his God, and wave his hand over the spot and cure the leprosy! Are not the rivers of Damascus better than all the waters of Israel? Could I not wash in them, and be clean?" He turned and went away in a rage. Ultimately, <u>Naaman's servants had to convince him</u> to do what the messenger of Elisha told him, and he was cured.

I do not know if we are dealing with excessive pride or what, but I do know that we Americans have since the initial request fought World War II, the Korean War, the Vietnam War, two wars in Iraq, and a war in Afghanistan, with many soldiers lost or wounded and Russia has not been converted. Also we have experienced the 9-11 devastation.

We must demand obedience to the Mother of God. If the Bishops are the problem, we will request to de-frock the sick ones. If the Pope is the problem, we will request his resignation. Since we have had a number of popes since Mary made this request through the Fatima's Lucia, I would suspect the big problem is with the Bishops. However, the Pope may not be taking the correct action in fear of a big scandal. It is more important to be obedient to Mary, the Mother of God, then to worry about some potential scandal.

This will be our priority number one activity in our war against sin. They are setting up very bad example to all the Christian faithful.

2 | Background

Back in the late 1970s, the Lord told me, He was giving me many experiences to develop my leadership abilities and that when I turn eighty years of age, He will call on me to be a twenty-first century Moses.

On the morning of April 24, 2014, the Lord reminded me of my upcoming eightieth birthday on August 20 of this year. He left me that impression that I ought to study Moses' history as related in the second book of the Bible entitled "Exodus."

Exodus relates the story of God's miraculous rescue of the Israelites. He brought these descendents of Jacob out of the Egyptian slavery via His chosen leader, Moses. Moses led the newly freed people across the Red Sea to Mount Sinai, where they entered into a special covenant with the Lord.

This covenant was the extension of the partnership God made with Abraham. God gave Abraham along with his descendents the whole land of Canaan, with the condition that Abraham's offspring keep God's commandments.

God called Moses of the Old Testament against his will, for Moses said: "If you please Lord, send someone else!" (Exodus, Chapter 4, verse 13)

During the Last Supper Jesus told His disciples: "It was not you who chose me, but I who chose you and appointed you to go and bear fruit that will remain…" (John, Chapter 15, verse 16)

Now the Father has called me, Bernard C. Rauckhorst to be the twenty-first century Moses. I believe He chose me, because of my special relationship to God the Father's Daughter, God the Son's Mother and God the Holy Spirit's Spouse, Mary.

Jesus in His 30 years of hidden life elevated Mary to the Pinnacle of Sanctity, far exceeding the Angels in heaven. It is this Lady who can cure our present day society of the slavery of sin. Just as Jesus Christ is our mediator with the Father, He has appointed the most Blessed Virgin, His Mother and our Mother to be the Mediatrix of All Grace.

Mary's title of the Immaculate Conception was dogmatized in 1854 by Pope Pius the IX. Her title "Mary, Mediatrix of all Grace" should be dogmatized in near future. It is probably being held up due to the pharisaic scandal it will cause for some of our brother Christians.

Mary gave us the answer to our current world problem when she said: "Jesus wants to establish in the world devotion to My Immaculate Heart. I promise salvation to those who embrace it, and their souls will be loved by God, as flowers placed by myself to adorn His throne." (From Blessed Virgin Mary at Fatima, June 13, 1917)

To obtain Her help, Our Lady asks only for prayer, sacrifice, reparation and consecration. So this shall be the endeavor of the 21st-century Moses to establish universal devotion to Mary's Immaculate Heart.

There are two ways that I pray to yours and my Father. The first way is as a child. When I say the Our Father at Mass, I extend my arms like a child who desires his mother or dad to pick him up and embrace him. The second way is I abandon myself into His hands and ask Him to do with me what He wills (See Appendix I).

So this book is going to be a plan, inspired by heavenly people, to fight and win the war against sin.

The old Moses had his Princes, but I will have my generals because we are going to war. These leaders may be male or female. In the 20th-century, we saw an outstanding female leader Mother Theresa and another who extends into the 21st-century named Mother Angelica.

As soon as this book is published, it will be distributed initially to chosen people, the generals who will lead in fighting the battles. It will also be sent to our Holy Father, Pope Francis and some to the American Bishops. Subsequently I will request that Pope Francis:

1. United with the Bishops Consecrate Russia to Mary's Immaculate Heart and
2. Dogmatize the title of Mary, "Mary, Mediatrix of All Grace."

If the pope would take these actions, he would bring Our Mother Mary, to the forefront of the world, exactly where she belongs.

When the birthday of the Church occurred on Pentecost, the Holy Spirit came with power, wind and fire. I will appeal to our Heavenly Father to increase the Holy Spirit within us, and ask Him to demolish some billboards and theatres that have been blasphemous to His Spouse in acknowledgement of my appointment as the twenty-first century Moses.

Remember we have God on our side, always. He is in us and with us.

In the course of this book, I will describe certain ways of prayer, such as asking for increases in the gifts of Faith, Hope, and Charity during the first three Hail Marys of the Rosary. I know our generals are aware of this tradition, but I am hoping that our efforts will bring many new recruits into our war on sin that may choose to read this book.

3

The People

The Lord made a covenant with Abraham and his descendents and specifically with Abraham's son Isaac. But God told Abraham his descendents would be enslaved and oppressed for four hundred years. (Genesis: Chapter 15, verse 13)

Isaac had a son named Jacob. The covenant included him too and subsequently his twelve sons. From those twelve sons came the twelve tribes of the Jewish nation. These sons had their own children and when a famine arrived Jacob's family moved to Egypt. They were seventy strong not counting the wives of Jacobs sons. The group and their offspring lived in Egypt for four hundred years before God freed them through Moses.

Now in the first-century A.D. Jesus made a new covenant with the offspring of Abraham, Isaac, Jacob, and Judah. The people of this new covenant are known as Christians.

They believe Jesus is the son of God and they have been baptized into the body of Jesus (which is necessary for salvation).

Jesus gave his people two all encompassing Commandments. They are: "You shall love the Lord, your God, with all your heart, with all your soul, and with all your mind" and the second is "You shall love your neighbor as yourself." (Matthew, Chapter 22, verses 37 through 40)

Each group of people has not been living up to the standards of decency.

In the case of Jacob's sons, they were murderers; they sold their brother into slavery, and in one case slept with his father's concubine.

In the case of the Christians we can enumerate many offenses against God and man, for instance aborting 40 million babies per year in our world and the lack of attendance at Sunday Worship services.

The Jewish people were always complaining starting with Abram. When God told him, "I will make your reward very great," he said: "O Lord God what good will gifts be, if I keep on being childless and have as my heir the steward of my house, Eliezer?" (Genesis: Chapter 15, verses 1 and 2)

The twenty-first century Christians are also always complaining, saying: "Why me Lord?" at the first sign of a problem.

In Moses' time the Jewish people were hated by the Egyptians and seemingly have been hated ever since.

The initial Christian leader, "Christ," was murdered on the cross and His followers severely suffered persecution for the next several hundred years and still do in certain parts of the globe.

So there is a similarity between the Jewish people and the Christians in many facets of life.

4 | Slavery

A King came into power in Egypt who had a fear of the Jewish people, since they were very fertile and growing in population faster than the Egyptians. So he placed them under forced labor and tried to reduce the Jewish male inhabitants by killing them at birth.

We Christians have a volunteer slavery in our country of the United States of America. It is called a slavery of "sin." Approximately 40% of youngsters have obtained sexual diseases by being promiscuous. Our divorce rate is at about 50%. A new large portion of the population is into what is called, "same sex marriages." We now have an abnormal death rate due to overdosing on drugs. The list goes on.

So the Jewish people of Moses' time were forced into slavery and the 21st century Moses finds his Christian people in a volunteer slavery of sin.

5

Moses: First and Second

The Lord looks out for specific people in special ways. The first Moses was born to parents of Levi tribe. At that time, the Egyptian king had given the order to kill all male children born to Hebrew women.

His mother hid him for the first three months of his life. Then she decided she could not hide him any longer, and placed him in a basket that she covered with bitumen and pitch to make it waterproof. Then she placed the child among the reeds on the riverbank. Moses' sister Miriam stationed herself at a distance to see what would happen to him.

Pharaoh's daughter came down to the river to bathe and noticing the basket among the reeds and sent her handmaiden to retrieve it. Subsequently, she was moved for pity for him. Miriam asked pharaoh's daughter if she could find a Hebrew woman to nurse the child for her. In this manner Moses was given back to his natural mother for the first three years of his life.

Living in the household of the pharaoh's daughter, it would be reasonable believe that he received adequate food, clothing and the best education available at that time. On one occasion after Moses had grown up, he visited his kinsman and witnessed their forced labor. He saw an Egyptian striking a Hebrew. Looking about and seeing no one, he killed the Egyptian and hid him in the sand.

The secrecy of this affair was short-lived and he became a wanted man, so he fled to the land of Midian.

Ultimately, he was given a wife from a priest with seven daughters for protecting them while they watered their flock. Her name was Zipporah and she gave Moses two sons Gershom and Eliezer.

Many years later Moses was called to be God's instrument in freeing the Hebrews from Egyptian slavery. He is now about 80 years old and he is answering God, "Who am I, that I should go to Pharaoh and lead the Israelites out of Egypt?"

God said, "I will be with you."

But Moses said to God, "When I go to the Israelites and say to them, the God of your fathers has sent me to you; if they ask me "What is his name?' What am I to tell them?"

God then said you shall tell the Israelites: "I Am sent me to you."

"But," Moses objected, "suppose they'd will not believe me, nor listen to my plea? For they may say, The Lord did not appear to you."

Then the Lord gave him several miracles he could employ, first his staff could be changed into a serpent and back into a staff. Second his hand could be leprous and then healthy again. Third he could take water from the river and poured onto the ground and by doing this; the water would change into blood.

Moses however, said that the Lord, "If you please, Lord, I have never been eloquent, neither in the past, nor recently, nor now that you have spoken to your servant: but I am slow of speech and tongue."

But the Lord told him, "Go then! It is I who will assist you in speaking and will teach you what you are to say."

Moses then said, "If you please, Lord, send someone else!"

Now the Lord became angry with Moses and said He would make his brother Aaron the spokesman and told Moses "You shall be as God to him."

I, the twenty-first century Moses was also the baby of my family, having two older brothers and two older sisters. My parents were good people giving public worship on all Sundays and holy days. They sent all their children to Immaculate Conception grammar school and St. Mary's high school. In my case my father encouraged me to go to John Carroll University. I did and attained a degree in

Natural Science. In our household the rosary was a very prevalent prayer.

Like the old Moses, I was fed well, clothed adequately, and given an opportunity for an excellent education.

I married my sweetheart, Alice Fuerst, a month after getting my degree from John Carroll University, and subsequently sired seven children Peggy, Laura, Valerie, Bernard, Martin, Therese, and Diane. My wonderful wife of fifty-four years left for heaven in May of 2010 and is now one of my heavenly workers.

Just like the original Moses, I am not an eloquent speaker. Once, when I had to give a technical presentation with 10 other people, I was relaxing at a bar thinking "Thank God that is over with."

Just then my boss came up to me and told me the people in charge wanted to hear my presentation again first thing in the morning. Then he added that my presentation was the only one that sounded like it came from an engineer. The rest of the presentations sounded like they came from salesman.

So my boss talked like my lack of eloquence in this case was an asset.

I also share the same fear that the first Moses displayed, but our Heavenly Father has already given me a Nation to be in charge of upon our bodily resurrection. So I am inebriated with His infinite love and will not let it be a handicap in the pursuit of His goals.

Since we are now involved in a different type of slavery, now the staff will be replaced by the rosary.

The first Moses was to lead his people to the promise land, "Canaan;" and the second Moses to the promise land, heaven.

6

Intimacy With God

In Chapter 33 of Exodus, starting at verse 12, Moses said to the Lord, "You indeed, are telling me to lead this people on; but you have not let me know whom you will send with me. Yet you have said, 'You are my intimate friend,' and also, 'You have found favor with me.' Now, if I have found favor with you, do let me know your ways so that, in knowing you, I may continue to find favor with you. Then, too, this nation is, after all, your own people."

"I myself," the Lord answered, "will go a long, to give you rest."

Moses replied, "If you are not going yourself, do not make us go up from here. For how can it be known that we, your people and I, have found favor with you, except by you going with us? Then we your people and I will be singled out from every other people on earth."

The Lord said to Moses, "This request, too, which you have just made, I will carry out, because you have found favor with me and you are my intimate friend."

As noted in the Introduction Chapter of *My Country of the Heavenly Queen*, the Lord has found favor with the 21st century Moses by putting him in charge of a portion of heaven upon the resurrection of the body. He did this for my endeavors to promote Jesus' mother as our greatest advocate, the refuge of sinners, Mother of Divine Mercy, and Mother of Perpetual Help.

It is with my intimacy with Mary the Mother of God that has now led to my intimacy with our Heavenly Father. It is for this reason He has made me the new Moses, because he knows that I recognize that Mary is the solution to today's slavery problem.

7
The End of Slavery for the Israelites

Moses and Aaron went to Pharaoh and said, "Thus says the Lord, the God of Israel: Let my people go, that they may celebrate a feast to me in the desert." Because God knew the king of Egypt would not allow them to go unless he was forced.

In his initial objection, Pharaoh decided the Hebrews should work harder in their slavery and made their jobs more demanding.

In the process to win their freedom, the Lord sent plagues on the Egyptians. These were:

1. Turning their water into blood.
2. Covered the area with frogs.
3. Sent gnats throughout the land.
4. Sent swarms of flies upon them.

Pharaoh gave them permission to celebrate a feast to their God during the second, fourth, seventh and eighth plagues, but reneged as soon as the frogs, flies, hail, and locust disappeared.

5. Sent a pestilence on their livestock causing death.
6. Sent a plague of boils on their people.
7. Sent a hailstorm.

8. Sent a plague of locusts.
9. Sent out three days of darkness.
10. The "first-born" died.

It was only after the death of all the first born Egyptians and their first born animals did the Pharaoh once again give the Hebrews permission to take their animals and leave this land to worship their God.

The Lord preceded them, in the daytime by means of a column of cloud to show the way, and at night time by means of a column of fire to give them light. Thus they could travel both day and night.

Then the Pharaoh changed his mind and sent 600 first-class chariots plus others, armed warriors, to bring them back as slaves once again.

This time Moses stretched out his hand over the Red Sea and the Lord parted the waters with walls on the right and left sides and the wind to dry the bottom area. Thus the Israelites marched into the midst of the sea on dry land and crossed safely to the other side. The Egyptian army which had followed the Israelites into the sea all perished when Moses stretched out his hands over the sea, so that water flowed back upon the Egyptians.

So now the Hebrews were freed from the Egyptian slavery. They were extremely happy singing and dancing in praise of God.

This activity was short-lived, for Moses marched them out to the desert of Shur. After traveling for three days through the desert without finding water, they arrived at Marah, were they could not drink the water, because it was too bitter. So people grumbled against Moses, saying, "What are we to drink?" Moses in turn appealed to the Lord, who instructed him how to make the water fresh.

Shortly, their travels took them to the desert of Sin. Again the Israelite community grumbled against Moses, complaining "You lead us into this desert to make the whole community die of famine."

Again Moses appealed to the Lord, and God sent them manna, bread from heaven, for their morning rations and Quail, meat for their evening meal.

Next they journeyed to Rephidim and again there was no water, causing more complaining by the Hebrews saying, "Is the Lord in our midst or not?" The Lord instructed Moses to strike the rock with his staff and the water problem disappeared.

Then Amalek came and waged war against Israel and Moses was on top of the hill with the staff of God raised over his head and Joshua, his general, mowed down, Amalek and his people. The Lord said, "I will completely block out the memory of Amalek from under the heavens."

Recognizing when Hebrews initially arrived in Egypt, there were approximately 100 people counting wives and concubines. The 400 years would result in approximately twelve generations. Assuming they doubled in size each generation, the population when they were freed would exceed 400,000 people; but according to the census there were 603,550 males of 20 years or older not counting women or children.

Now Jethro, Moses' father-in-law, the priest of Midian arrived to visit Moses and gave him some good advice, telling him to appoint judges to handle all the minor problems with the people, so that he would not wear himself out settling every problem.

After the third month of their departure from the land of Egypt they came to the desert of Sinai. It is here at the Lord gave them the Ten Commandments, laws regarding slaves, personal injury, property damage, trusts and loans, social laws and religious laws. All these would be related to the Hebrews by Moses.

Then the Lord told Moses to take a collection from the people so an ark could be made, a sanctuary for God. The Lord then gave Moses a complete description on how it was to be made including all of the contents along with the priestly vestments.

When Moses came down off the mountain with all God's instructions along with the two tablets containing the Ten Commandments inscribed by God's own finger, he found them worshiping a molten calf saying, "This is your God, O Israel who brought you out of the land of Egypt." This kind of behavior seemed to prevail for years through King Solomon and beyond.

The Lord was ready to consume them into death but Moses stayed his hand and the Lord relented and his punishment he had threatened to inflict on his people.

8

The New Moses Plan in General

One of the Legion of Mary's prayers starts out with the following words:

> "Confer, O Lord, on us, who serves beneath the standard of Mary, the fullness of faith in you and trust in her, to which it is given to conquer the world."

This is exactly task of the new Moses, to deliver the people from the slavery of sin, which is to conquer the world.

In *The True Story of Fatima*, Mary gives the answer to solve our slavery problem. She asks only for prayer, sacrifice, reparation and consecration.

Speaking about those who help Her and who are devoted to Her Immaculate Heart, Our Lady solemnly promised:

> "These souls will be loved by God, as flowers placed by Myself to adorn His throne."

So we know the basic solution to the problem and the great reward for all those people who fully participate in making it happen.

The method that Jesus gave us was the initial 12 apostles, each with different talents. In the book *The Mystical City of God*, when

James the brother of John went to convert Spain he also took twelve disciples with him.

I believe we could organize the twelve existing Marian groups (without them losing their autonomy). The groups would share some common actions. These groups will be (See Appendix II):

1. America Needs Fatima
2. Apostles of the Holy Spirit
3. Association of Mary and Helpers
4. Association of the Miraculous Medal
5. Caritas of Birmingham (An Advocate of Medjugorje)
6. Franciscan Missionaries of the Eternal Word (EWTN)
7. Legion of Mary
8. Marianist Missions
9. Marionhill Fathers
10. Oblate Mission (An Advocate of Our Lady of Guadalupe)
11. The Fatima Center
12. World Apostolate of Fatima (Our Lady's Blue Army)

I think we could promote at all of the Masses of these organizations, one special petition to be said along with all their other petitions for an indefinite period of time. This is: "We consecrate Russia to Mary's Immaculate Heart, we pray."

Vatican II, named Mary, "Mother of the Church." So by this petition, we are showing obedience to one of the Fatima requests and acknowledging Her power.

Back in World War II, our pastor would always say the "Prayer to St. Michael" at the conclusion of Mass, so there is a precedent in saying a prayer for an indefinite period.

Next, one Hail Mary would be appropriate right after the petitions. This seems quite common with some of the priests right now that say Mass on EWTN. Our objective is to make it permanent, for Mary is permanently the Mother of the Church.

"America Needs Fatima" sponsors a "Public Square Rosary Rally Crusade" annually in October, which is an excellent promotion but maybe we could prevail on them or another organization to promote one in May, the month of Mary, the month of mothers.

One of the problems that now exist is: the "Fatima story" is not spoken about to any extent. It has been stifled by the clergy and/or educators. This has to be rectified. It seems that certain people are carrying the devil in their pocket, willingly or not. We should try to get knowledgeable people to promote the story of Fatima in the seminaries as a starting point.

When the Lord started His church He also sent the Holy Spirit to enlighten His workers as well as sending the Holy Spirit to the newly Baptized. All of the leaders that we will depend on to change the world will have been Baptized and Confirmed, thus having received the Holy Spirit. It is my contention that our leaders should pray to the Holy Spirit in a perpetual Novena. There are probably many different novenas to the Holy Spirit two are:

1. *The Holy Spirit* by the Franciscan Mission Associates, PO Box 598, Mount Vernon, New York 0598.
2. *Novena to The Holy Spirit, Help me to Know You* by George E. Schulhoff A.H.S., Apostles of the Holy Spirit, 2709 Woodburn Avenue, Cincinnati, Ohio 45206.

Or a Daily Prayer to the Holy Spirit such as:

> Breathe in me, O Holy Spirit,
> That my thoughts,
> May all be holy;
> Act in me, O Holy Spirit,
> That my work too,
> May be holy;
> Draw my heart, O Holy Spirit,
> That I love but what is holy;
> Strengthen me, O Holy Spirit,
> To defend all that is holy:
> Guard me then, O Holy Spirit,
> That I always may be holy.
>   St. Augustine
>   (354-430 AD)

Our Lady of Medjugorje said to the children on January 25, 1987, "Dear children, behold, also today I want to call you to start living a new life as of today. Dear children, I want you to comprehend that God has chosen each one of you, in order to use you in a great plan for the solution of mankind…"

I change her "children" to "Jonahs" and apply it to the world's people (for we need much help).

Regarding our "Jonahs" to preach penance, the first and foremost activity is to say and promote the daily rosary for the reparation of sins against the Sacred Heart of Jesus and the Immaculate Heart of Mary. Our Jonahs would begin rotating twenty-seven days in petition and then twenty-seven days in thanksgiving. Note the nice reflection on the Devotion to Mary by Darlene M. O'Sullivan in Appendix III.

One very practical activity our generals could promote is all night vigils. These vigils which are performed with the exposed Blessed Sacrament can start and end with Mass or start with the procession with the Eucharist and end with the Mass. In between, a number of five decade rosaries can be said, along with confessions, songs, readings, and Consecration to Mary Immaculate (See Appendix IV).

If we could initially get our twelve generals to sign up for one vigil a year, it would be a good start. But there is no reason, that each general could recruit twelve captains with each organizing one all night vigil per month in their geographical area, so that by the second year we could be up to one hundred and forty-four.

If we can promote an adequate number of vigils, where we give up a night of sleep while consecrating ourselves to the Immaculate Heart of Mary while reciting a number of rosaries, I think we can conquer the world.

Note that vigils incorporate all four items Mary requested, prayer, sacrifice, reparation and consecration.

Our Lady of Fatima during the Miracle of the Sun on October 13, 1917, held out the Brown Scapular. She wants us to wear the scapular always and say five decades of the Most Holy Rosary each day. Many of us old timers were invested in the Confraternity of the Brown Scapular the day after our first Holy Communion.

9

The Devil Problems

In order to discredit Moses, Pharaoh's magicians replicated some of Moses' plagues by using their magic arts. These included:

1. The magicians threw their staffs to the ground and the staffs turned into snakes.
2. The magicians were able to make some water appear to change into blood.
3. The magicians made frogs overrun Egypt.

These activities do not seem like human activities since they were hindering God of freeing his people. The reasonable conclusion is they were devils.

As a youngster in eighth grade, at the end of Mass our Pastor turned and lit into our Principal, a nun probably in her late fifties, in front of the whole student body (approximately 240 children). It is one of my biggest regrets in life that I did not walk up to him and tell him he was out of line. I was lacking the courage or fortitude that is why I recommend a perpetual novena to the Holy Spirit. I believe he was carrying a devil in his hip pocket without him realizing it.

Thirty years later, I was at a "Day of Recollection" and went out of the church for smoke. A lady just started talking and told me how she left the church many years ago because of something that happened with that same pastor. She still seemed bitter and I think it is safe to say that she had not fully forgiven that priest. If I would've had the courage to stand up against him in the eighth grade I might have prevented this lady's problem and possibly many more.

In a correspondence from father Nicholas Gruner of the Fatima Center, Father Gruner said, "some very powerful people, in effect, lowered a blanket of silence over the true story and message of Fatima. If Fatima is not spoken about, they hope it will be forgotten!" Note the Church has designated May 13 as Our Lady of Fatima day and seven Popes have approved the Fatima story. If Father Gruner is right, then I would consider we have some people walking around with a devil in their pocket, with or without their knowledge, and they need to be confronted. Father Gruner's use of the word "powerful" may suggest Bishops.

In a correspondence from Rev. Richard P. McBrien[1] regarding the teaching authority of the Church, Rev. McBrien states: "There is an even broader meaning of teaching authority in the Church, namely, the teaching authority inherent in and exercised by every member of the Church. It is known simply as the magisterium of the whole Church, the Ecclesia docens ("the teaching Church"), and is rooted in Baptism.

In the past, the term *Ecclesia docens* was limited to the hierarchy, while the rest of the faithful including theologians, were considered the *Ecclesia disens* ("the learning Church"). With Vatican II, that distinction disappeared.

There is a story of the Great Saint Bernard who was a proficient writer as well as a founder of monasteries, who lived in the 12th century. Although, the seventh century Eastern Church began to observe the feast of the Immaculate Conception of the Blessed Virgin Mary on December 8th, St. Bernard five centuries later denied the Immaculate Conception of Mary. It is said, he appeared to some lady after his death, showing a stain on his forehead and telling her that he got the stain because he had stated that the Virgin Mary was conceived in Original Sin.

It does seem likely that he could've had the devil in his hip pocket and not have known it. St. Bernard did many good works, but taking the stand that Mary was not Immaculately conceived shows that the devil was around and active.

---

[1] Fr. Richard McBrien
   a. Wrote a weekly column for forty-five years (2,364 in all) titled "Essays in Theology."
   b. He was President of the Catholic Theological Society of America.
   c. He taught at Notre Dame University for thirty years and was the chair of their Theology Department for eleven years,
   d. And much more.

10

Incomprehensible Behavior

The Lord freed the Israelite people from slavery through the actions of Moses. They were given water, manna and quail from heaven. But still the Israelites made a golden calf and cried out, "This is your God, O Israel who brought you out of the land of Egypt." The fact they did this is incomprehensible.

Likewise, any Catholic clergy that disbelieves or hinders the promotion of the Fatima story is incomprehensible to me. The Fatima apparition has been approved by the Catholic Church and seven Popes. But apparently, it is happening. It is true that I have not heard a sermon at mass regarding Our Lady of Fatima or read about Fatima in a parish bulletin in recent years.

11

The Tribes of the Israelites

One year after the Israelites departure from Egypt the Lord told Moses to take a census of all the men who were twenty years or older who were fit for military service. To assist in this activity, one man from each tribe, the head of his ancestral house, also known as the tribal prince aided in the census. The results were:

Tribe of Reuben	--	46,500
Tribe of Simeon	--	59,300
Tribe of Gad	--	45,650
Tribe of Judah	--	74,600
Tribe of Issachar	--	54,400
Tribe of Zebulun	--	57,400
Tribe of Joseph (Ephraim)	--	40,500
Tribe of Manasseh	--	32,200
Tribe of Benjamin	--	35,400
Tribe of Dan	--	62,700
Tribe of Asher	--	41,500
Tribe of Naphtali	--	53,400

Note the total number of men 20 years or older for all the tribes, not counting the Levites who were the priestly Tribe was 603,550. (Numbers: Chapter 1, verses 20 through 46)

Just as the Old Testament is a prelude to the New Testament,

Moses and the twelve tribes were a prelude to Jesus and the twelve apostles.

Now there will be a twenty-first century Moses, with twelve organizations. The organizations' lay supporters will be numbered in the thousands and probably total over several million although some people will be associated with more than one organization. So we have a sizable army but it is lean compared to our adversaries.

Now Moses sent one man from each of 10 tribes and two from the Joseph Tribe negating the Tribe of Levi to reconnoiter the land of Canaan, all tribal princes for forty days.

When they returned only two Israelites were ready to go capture the land, with all the others displaying great fear. Again, they negated that the All-Powerful Lord would be on their side. For this, they paid a great price, another 40 years roaming the desert; with none of the fearful people seeing the Promised Land.

Now when we initiate this plan and of the 21st century Moses, God is backing it. He wants to see an optimistic, solidified group (army) of our twelve organizations using the rosary as our main weapon.

12

Weekly Worship

Do you ever think about the number of people that touch your life? When the alarm clock rings in the morning, do you sit up, shut the alarm off, and turn a light on? Note:

1. Someone made the alarm clock.
2. It was packed and transported to a store by some people.
3. Then it was priced and displayed by someone.
4. Finally, you purchased it from a cashier.
5. You turn the light on because someone wired your house. A generator was required to make that happen. Someone had to build the generator. It is powered by coal or another source of energy. Coal for example requires a number of workers to retrieve and transport.
6. If you are sitting on a bed made of wood, someone cut down the trees, another cut log into the boards, and another had to transport them. Some craftsman had to turn the wood into a bed. Again, it had to be packed and shipped to the store where it was displayed and priced. After you purchased this bed it had to be delivered and assembled in your residence.
7. The bed was useless without a mattress, springs, sheets and blankets.
8. Think about the source of your pajamas, the hot water in your shower, your toothbrush and shaving equipment.

You have been up fifteen minutes and already a thousand people have touched your life. That is why we are called social beings.

Think about when we have a storm and the electricity goes out. No lights, no TV, no coffee, no toast, no refrigeration, no working traffic lights, as a result of one act of God.

If you love someone, you like to be around them. Can you visualize a husband who would not be seen with his wife outside the house? Would it not send a message, that he is ashamed of her?

Private prayer is good, but the value of it when not accompanying it in a social atmosphere would appear to be next to nil. It's like you are ashamed to admit you love God in front of your brothers and sisters.

One hour a week of worshiping your God in conjunction with your neighbors seems a very reasonable request. It is why it is a serious obligation for all Catholics and should be for all Christians.

13

The Boring Mass

When less than thirty percent of our Catholics attend Sunday Mass, this is a significant problem. Especially when one considers that the Church calls the Mass the source and summit of the Christian life. The Church also makes going to Sunday Mass a serious obligation.

What we get out of Mass is associated with what we and our co-churchgoers bring to Mass and often this is very lacking. I believe the basic problem is ignorance and it results in a boring experience. One way I believe we could start educating our youth is by incorporating dancing in the Mass at three distinct times. These would be:

1. At the entrance to Mass
2. When the gifts are carried to the altar
3. After Communion

Consider the first case. When the Bible, the Word of God, is being carried down the aisle, this is a reason to be excited. In a few minutes the Word of God is going to be proclaimed. Jesus is going to speak to each person in attendance. It is like David dancing before the Ark when it was brought to Jerusalem. The entrance music should change to something lively to recognize the excitement about what is going to take place.

At the time the gifts are brought up, there are supposed to be the same number of hosts as people present. Symbolically, the whole congregation is coming forward to place themselves on the altar. All present are "presenting their body as a living sacrifice," to be offered <u>with</u> Christ and <u>in</u> Christ during the Eucharistic prayer.

This seems to be a logical place to have a group of people showing excitement about offering themselves with Christ. When this new protocol is explained in the Sunday bulletin it will add a layer of education to the congregation.

Many years ago, I observed gals dancing after Communion in the Catholic Church in Hawaii. Again, it is a happy time for the congregation after receiving the Body, Blood, Soul, and Divinity of Jesus Christ.

The implementation of including dancing in the Mass should be with a two-fold objective. First it will be to educate in general and secondly it will increase each individual's physical, mental, and spiritual participation.

It is probably unrealistic to attempt to incorporate all three dances at once. They could be added one at a time until all three are added.

Note, Psalm 149: verse 3 states: "Let them praise his name in festive dance…"

14

Abortion

It is estimated that "forty million" abortions are performed annually on our planet.

"Hear the word of the Lord princes of Sodom! Listen to the instruction of our God, people of Gomorrah!...Your hands are full of blood!" (Isaiah 1:10-15)

Remember the fifth commandment that God gave His people through the Old Testament Moses.

"Thou shall not kill!" (Exodus 20:13)

What is the difficulty in understanding this commandment?

With abortion, the mother is allowing her own flesh and blood to be terminated; how sad.

How many geniuses have we lost via abortion that would have discovered the cause of Alzheimer's disease and then the method of preventing the ailment or the causes of a number of types of cancers along with the methods of prevention?

Is there any problem of understanding our need for millions of "Jonas" to preach penance?

15

Mary the Refuge of Sinners

Mary, Immaculate Conception conceived without sin, experienced the effects of sin when Jesus separated himself from his parents as told in Chapter 2 of Luke's Gospel; for serious sin separates us from God. It was because of this terrible experience that she understands the plight of sinners and she has now been given the title of "Refuge of Sinners." So, in order to solve the "Slavery of Sin" problem, She is and always will be the starting point.

It is interesting that Jesus spent the first 30 years of his life in the total work of bringing Mary to the pinnacle of sanctity, compared to only three years in forming His Church as told in the book the *Mystical City of God* written by Mary of Agreda, translated by Fiscar Mariso from Spanish to English. The book describes the Divine History and the Life of the Virgin Mother of God.

The *Mystical City of God* goes into so much detail in its four volumes and it is a gold mine of the hidden life of Jesus. The book was so closely scrutinized by those in authority and afterwards. It has been approved by Innocent IX, Alexander VIII, Clement IX, Benedict XIII, and Benedict XIV.

My American people are not used to wading through a lot of boring information for example:

"I confess to Thee and magnify Thee, King Most High, that in Thy exalted Majesty Thou has hidden these high mysteries from the wise and from the teachers, and in Thy condescension hast revealed them to me, the most insignificant and useless slave of Thy Church, in order that Thou mayest be the more admired as the omnipotent Author of this history in proportion as its instrument is despicable and weak."

These kinds of paragraphs are littered throughout the book making the mining for gold more time-consuming which is difficult for our people of instant gratification.

From Luke, Chapter 1, Mary was the instrument of Elizabeth receiving the Holy Spirit and the sanctification of John the Baptist in Elizabeth's womb and gave Zachariah his voice back. Mary, according to the *Mystical City of God*, worked many hidden miracles throughout her lifetime on earth.

Jesus taught Mary the Gospels before they were written; and also the seven sacraments before they were instituted in preparation for her being the Mother of the Church. This Motherhood was accomplished when Jesus was on the cross and He said to His Mother, "Woman, behold your son." The he said to the disciple John, "Behold your mother." (John: Chapter 19, verses 26 and27)

According to the *Mystical City of God*, regarding the death of Herod as noted in Acts, Chapter 12, verses 20-24, Mary requested that the Most High to prevent Herod from executing his designs for the destruction of the Church. The Lord told Mary, She should execute sentence on Herod. She stated, "She never calls for vengeance but only desired their salvation if possible. God told her, the man will accept no help and is destined for hell. She answered that He has granted her to be the Refuge of Sinners, the Advocate and Intercessor of Sinners. The Lord told her that is true for mortals who wish to avail themselves of thy powerful intercession. She executed the sentence of death in order that Herod would not incur greater torments by executing the evil he had planned. Mary sent an angel to dispatch this evil man.

The Almighty wishes it to be understood that she possesses full power of judging all men and that all should honor Her, just as they honor her Son, as His true Mother. He has given Her the same power with Him in degree and proportion due to Her as His Mother.

16

The Rosary

After the Mass, there is no other prayer as powerful as the rosary. Mary told the children of Fatima:

1. On May 13, 1917, pray the Rosary every day
2. On June 13, 1917, pray the Rosary everyday
3. On July 13, 1917, continue praying the Rosary every day
4. On August 19, 1917, continue praying the Rosary every day
5. On September 13, 1917, continue to say the Rosary every day
6. On October 13, 1917, I am Our Lady of the Rosary, continue to say the Rosary every day

In the Rosary you start off by making "the Sign of the Cross." This should remind you of your Baptism when you became the body of Jesus.

Next, you say the "Creed", where you state your belief in the fourteen articles of faith.

After the "Creed" you say one of six "Our Fathers." The other five precede the decades of the "Hail Mary's." In the "Our Father" you are worshiping Him, you are asking for your daily bread and you are asking for His forgiveness. (**See Appendix V for the prayers.**)

This prayer followed by three of the fifty-three "Hail Mary's." The "Hail Mary "starts out with the Archangel Gabriel's announcement to

Mary, followed by Saint Elizabeth's blessing, and then we asked Mary to pray for us sinners.

These first three "Hail Mary's" should be prayed with the intention to increase our Faith Hope and Charity. The three Theological virtues such as:

> *We/I* believe in You, help *our/my* lack of faith.
> *We/I* trust in You, help *our/my* lack of trust.
> *We/I* love You; help *our/my* lack of love.

These three Hail Mary's are followed by the first six "All Glory be to the Father, Son and Holy Spirit as it was in the beginning, is now and ever shall be, world without end.*" The "All Glory Be*" prayer precedes or ends each decade of the Rosary.

There are four sets of mysteries. These are known as the Joyful, Sorrowful, Glorious and Luminous mysteries.

As you pray the different sets of Mysteries you contemplate on five events, one during each decade. Example: The Joyful Mysteries are:

- The Annunciation
- The Visitation
- The Nativity
- The Presentation
- The Finding of the Child Jesus in the Temple

During the first Joyful Mystery you think about Archangel Gabriel appearing to Mary asking her to be the Mother of God, and Mary's positive response.

Then prior to the first Hail Mary, you should say or think of Angel Gabriel's salute to Mary. Before the second, Mary's positive answer, prior to the third, the conception of Jesus by the Holy Spirit. Then before the fourth, think about the humility of Jesus taking on our human nature and prior to that fifth, Jesus the Word made flesh. At the sixth Hail Mary contemplate Jesus in the Eucharist and prior to the seventh thank God for giving us Mary as example of motherhood of

God. Before the eighth Hail Mary thank God for allowing us to act as His mother, taking Him into our body and giving Him to His people. Before the ninth Hail Mary ask Him for His mercy and prior to the 10th tell Him you love Him with an everlasting love.

It is the above kind of thought you should develop when you say each decade of the Mysteries. It is also called "meditating on the Mysteries."

After each decade followed by the "All Glory Be*," you may add a request for a specific virtue such as:

> "We bind these buds [Hail Mary's] for a virtue of humility, love, detachment from the world, purity, and obedience to the will of God."

*Many just pray "Glory be…But this author prays All Glory be…"

17

The Bronze Serpent

On one of the trips of the Israelites when they set out on the road from the Red Sea, the people complained against God and Moses, "Why have you brought us up from Egypt to die in this desert, where there is no food or water? We are disgusted with this wretched food."

In punishment the Lord sent among his people poisonous saraph serpents, which bit the people; so that many died. Then the people came to Moses and said, "We have sinned and complaining against the Lord and you. Pray the Lord to take the serpents from us." So Moses prayed for the people and the Lord said to Moses, "Make a saraph and mount it on a pole, and if anyone who has been bitten looks at it, he will recover." Moses accordingly made a bronze serpent and mounted it on a pole and it had the effect as the Lord said.

According to the Archbishop Fulton J. Sheen [who is under review for canonization] many of the events in the Old Testament prefigure events in the New Testament. Just as the manna in the Old Testament prefigures the Eucharist, likewise the bronze serpent prefigures Christ on the cross. The serpent brought physical health to the Israelites and Jesus on the cross brings a spiritual health.

On each Rosary is a crucifix which presents Christ's arms extended to embrace you. His head tilted to kiss you and with a little imagination you can see blood flowing from his heart to purify you.

Now as you pray the rosary you could extend your arms for a number of Hail Mary's per each decade as a sign of reciprocating His love.

18

Our Nation - America [Nineveh]

We Need Jonahs

One of our founding Fathers and first President, George Washington, was quoted as saying: "It is impossible to govern rightly without God and the Bible."

Our country has legalized abortion, same-sex marriages, divorce with insignificant cause, etc. Our country has taken prayer out of schools and now is taking prayer away from chaplains. It is in the present direction of atheist Communism.

Per the National Tribune, Volumes 4 and 12, Mary the Mother of Christ appeared to George Washington at Valley Forge in 1777. During that bitter winter at Valley Forge, Gen. Washington prayed often for Divine assistance. As the leader of this great country, a country that would be dedicated to the Immaculate Conception of Mary, it was fitting that She should appear to him in an answer to his prayers... But lest you doubt me, read carefully George Washington's own words:

> "This afternoon, as I was sitting at this table engaged in preparing a dispatch, looking up I saw standing on opposite a singularly beautiful female, so astonished was I, for I'd given strict orders to be undisturbed. Presently, I heard a voice say: "Son of the Republic, look and learn!" While at the same time my visitor extended Her arm earnestly. Before me lay

spread on one vast plain all the countries of Europe, Asia, Africa, and America. I cast my eyes on America and beheld villages, towns and cities springing up one after another until the whole land was dotted with them. And from Africa an ill-omened spectre approached. I then saw an angel, wearing the word Union, place an American flag between the divided nation and say: "Remember, ye are brethren! Instantly the inhabitants laid down their weapons, and united around the National Standard."

There is more to the story foretelling world wars and another yet to come. But do you see a difference in our present leader who says we are not a Christian Nation and our founding father. You see a difference between King Solomon with a thousand women to lead him astray and our first president who had one wife, Martha.

The eleven tribes of Solomon's nation were stripped down to basically one tribe at Solomon's death. President Washington's country has grown from 13 states to 50 states over seven generations. Remember the story of Jonah and the conversion of Nineveh. It would appear to me that we should look at the world as Nineveh and each one of us as a Jonah and try to stay the hand of the Lord: For a prediction of several wars was part of the vision with the last war being described as nuclear.

19

The Prizes - Canaan / Heaven

When Lord gave the Israelites the land of Canaan, He gave them large cities that they did not build, with houses full of goods; also cisterns that they did not dig, with vineyards and olive groves that they did not plant.

The Lord gave this property to them, not because of their merits, but to keep a promise which He made to their fathers: Abraham, Isaac, and Jacob.

Then He told them: "Heed My Commandments which I enjoin on you today, loving and serving the Lord, your God with all your heart and all your soul, I will give this seasonal rain to your land, the early rain and the late rain, that you may have your grain, wine and oil to gather in; and I will bring forth grass in your fields for your animals. Thus you may eat your fill, truly of milk and honey."

Per the seventh chapter of Revelation, "the ones who have washed their robes and made them white in the blood of the Lamb who have survived the time of great distress will find heaven and eternal home."

"For this reason they stand before God's throne and worship him day and night in his temple. The one who sits in the throne will shelter them.

They will not hunger or thirst anymore, nor will the sun strike them.

For the Lamb who is in the center of the throne will shepherd them and lead them to springs of life giving water, and God will wipe away every tear from their eyes."

According to Paul's first letter to the Corinthians in Chapter 15, verses 51 through54, where he describes the resurrection event he said: "Behold, I tell you a mystery. We shall not all fall asleep, but we will all be changed in a blink of an eye, at the last trumpet. For the trumpet will sound, the dead will be raised incorruptible, and we shall be changed. For that which is corruptible must clothe itself with incorruptibility, and that which is mortal must clothe itself with immortality. And when this which is corruptible clothes with incorruptibility and this which is mortal clothes itself with immortality, then the word that is written shall come about: "Death is swallowed up in victory."

20

Our Leader's Requirements

All our leaders that are going to be the first line of offense should accept the "Peace Pledge Formulas" which is:

Dear Queen and Mother, who promised at Fatima to convert Russia and bring peace to all mankind, in reparation to thy Immaculate Heart for all my sins and of the whole world, I solemnly promise:

1. To offer up every day the sacrifices demanded by my daily duty;
2. To say part of the Rosary daily while meditating on the mysteries:

At the beginning and end of each mystery, three prayers should be said:

I. O my Jesus, forgive us our sins, save us from the fires of hell, lead all souls to heaven, especially those in most need of Your mercy. (Requested by Mary.)
II. My Jesus, we believe in You, we adore You, we trust in You, we love You. We beg pardon for those who do not believe in You, do not adore You, do not trust You and do not love You. (Requested by Mary.)

III. My Jesus please protect and save the unborn. (Due to the great number of abortions)

3. To where the scapular of Mount Carmel as profession of this promise and as an act of consecration to Thee. I shall renew this promise often, especially in moments of temptation.

Also, I believe since we are going to evolve twelve autonomous organizations, we should cooperate in their endeavors as much as possible; such as:

1. For "The Association of the Miraculous Medal," we could wear the medal and once a day say they're prayer as noted in the **Appendix VI**.
2. For "America Needs Fatima," we could become Captains for them or recruit for them. EWTN could give them some visibility as they do for the Right-to-Life's march on Washington in January.
3. Maybe the <u>Leaves</u> Magazine of the Marianhill Fathers could do two or three short stories during the course of the year on:

    I. The Fatima story in general
    II. The power of the Rosary
    III. The power of the Brown Scapular

This would aid the Fatima Center, America Needs Fatima, and the World Apostolate of Fatima.

21

The Bottom Line

I have asked our God to annihilate any number of theaters and billboards that have blasphemed Mary the Mother of God throughout the world within a month of the publishing of this book, to show that God has appointed me, Bernard C. Rauckhorst, the 21st century Moses.

Our first task, for my generals and I, is to get the Pope in union with the bishops of the world to be obedient to the Mother of the Church, and to consecrate Russia to Mary's Immaculate Heart.

The second task is to make Jonahs throughout the world via the power of the rosary.

Sister Lucia of Fatima speaks on the rosary:

"The Most Holy Virgin in these last times in which we live has given a new efficacy to the recitation of the Rosary to such an extent that there is no problem, no matter how difficult it is, whether temporal or above all, spiritual, in the personal life of each one of us, of our families, of the families of the world, or of religious communities, or even life of peoples and nations, that cannot be solved by the Rosary. There is no problem I tell you, no matter how difficult it is, that we cannot resolve by the prayer of the Holy Rosary.

With the holy Rosary, we will save ourselves, we will sanctify ourselves, we will console Our Lord and obtain the salvation of many souls."

The Rosary is our weapon.

In a message to Sister Mary Ephrem (from the Congregation of the Sisters of the Most Precious Blood of Jesus in Rone City, Indiana) Our Blessed Mother asked that she be known as *Our Lady of America, the Immaculate Virgin*. In subsequent message, Our Lady promised that greater miracles than those granted at Lourdes and Fatima would be granted here in America, the United States in particular, if we would do as she desires.

22

A Misunderstanding of Mary's Power

It seems that many Christians, Catholic and non-Catholic, have a lack of appreciation for the power of Mary, the Mother of God. They know that our Lord Jesus Christ is our Mediator with our Heavenly Father and feel very comfortable in addressing their needs to Jesus, and rightfully so.

In Chapter 15 of John verse 26, Jesus said: "When the Advocate comes to whom I will send you from the Father, the Spirit of Truth that proceeds from the Father, he will testify to me." Now through Baptism and Confirmation you have received the Holy Spirit and formed a love relationship to Jesus Christ, Son of the Heavenly Father.

But Jesus is offering his Mother to us, from the cross as our Mediator with Him per John, Chapter 19, verse 26: "When Jesus saw his mother and disciple whom he loved, he said to his mother, 'Woman behold, your son.'" Mother's have a natural love for their children.

Just as Jesus promised to send us the Holy Spirit, He is offering us His Mother.

An analogy of this advantage would be if Jesus is the guard at the checkpoint to the highway to heaven, He would stop you to check your credentials. But, if you were riding in Mary's limousine, He would wave it right by, non-stop.

23 | A Note to the Generals

Your job is to keep doing what you are doing, but try to aid the other leaders in their endeavors where it is reasonable and feasible.

It has come to my attention in my recent readings of events that have taken place that put two generals in a clash. It reminds me of Saint Thomas versus the other apostles after Jesus appeared to the ten.

It should be easy to visualize Saint Thomas thinking, *How could Jesus appear to this motley crew and not me? Matthew was once a tax collector and Jesus had to drive seven demons out of Mary Magdalene. Peter denied Jesus three times after bragging his faith could never be shaken.* Thomas' pride would not let him believe the Jesus' Resurrection and appearance to the Apostles would not include him.

On the other hand it is easy to visualize the other ten apostles feeling ticked because they feel they are being called liars [a feeling which would have persisted for a number of days.] After several days of putting up with Thomas' negative attitude, the apostles went to Peter and told Peter to dismiss Thomas from the group.

This caused Peter some anxiety, since he had yet to become the "Rock." To his credit, he took the problem to our Mother, Mary. Mary told him; "Go back and pray and everything will turn out for the Greater Glory of God." The above story is paraphrased from the *Mystical City of God*.

From the above action we are now called "Blessed" after Jesus appeared to Thomas, because we believe without seeing.

Mary gave us good advice; the answer to clashes is prayer.

Appendix I

The Prayer of Abandonment to God
By Charles de Foucauld

Father,
I abandon myself into your hands;
Do with me what you will.
Whatever you may do, I thank you.
I'm ready for all, I accept all.
Let only your will be done in me,
And in all your creatures.
I wish no more than this, O Lord.
Into your hands I commend my soul.
I offer it to you
With all the love of my heart,
For I love you, Lord,
And so need to give myself,
To surrender myself into your hands,
Without reserve,
And with boundless confidence,
For you are my Father.

Appendix II

Appointed Generals and Their Locations

1. **America Needs Fatima**
   Robert E. Ritchie, Executive Director
   PO Box 341, Hanover, PA 17331
   Phone number: 1-888-317-5571
   www.americaneedsfatima.org

2. **Apostles of the Holy Spirit**
   The Holy Spirit's Choice
   2709 Woodburn Avenue
   Cincinnati, OH 45206-1724
   Phone number: 1-513-961-1122
   www.aoths.org

3. **Association of Mary and Helpers**
   Fr. Michael Gaitley [MIC]
   Stockbridge, MA 01263
   Phone number: 1-800-671-2020
   www.marian.org

4. **Association of the Miraculous Medal**
   Fr. Oscar Lukefahr, C.M., Spiritual Director
   1811 West Saint Joseph Street
   Perryville, MO 63775-1598
   Phone numbers: 1-800-264-MARY (6279)
   1-573-547-2508
   www.amm.org

5. **Caritas of Birmingham**
   Mr. Wayne Weible
   100 Our Lady Queen of Peace Drive
   Sterret, AL 35147-9987
   Phone number: 1-205-672-2000
   www.caritasofbirmingham.org

6. **Franciscan Missionaries of the Eternal Word (EWTN)**
   Fr. Anthony Mary
   5821 Old Leeds Road
   Irondale, AL 35210-2164
   www.franciscamissionaries.com

7. **Legion of Mary**
   Mary, Queen of the Angels Praesidium
   Deacon Kevin Boudreaux
   St. Joseph Catholic Church
   11730 Old Saint Augustine Road
   Jacksonville, FL 32258
   http://mqangelspraesidium.com

8. **Marianist Missions – Mount Saint John**
   Fr. Patrick T. Tonry, S.M. - Spiritual Director
   4435 East Peterson Road
   Dayton, OH 45481-0001
   Phone number: 1-800-348-4732
   www.marianist.com/mission

9. **Marianhill Fathers**
   Rev. Thomas Heier, C.M.M.
   Editor-in-Chief of "Leaves"
   PO Box 87
   Dearborn MI 48121-0087
   Phone number: 1-313-561-2330
   www.marianhill.us

10. **Oblate Missions – Missionary Association of Mary Immaculate**
    Fr. Saturnino Lajo, O.M.I.
    323 Oblate Drive
    San Antonio, Texas 78216
    Phone number: 1-210-736-1685

11. **The Fatima Center – Servants of Jesus and Mary**
    Fr. Nicholas Gruner
    17000 State Route 30
    Constable, NY 12926
    Telephone number: 1-800-263-8160
    www.oblatemissions.org

12. **World Apostolate of Fatima, USA**
    Fr. Paul Ruge, Shrine Chaplain
    PO Box 976
    Washington, NJ 07882
    Phone number: 1-908-689-1700
    www.bluearmy.com

Appendix III

Devotion to Mary
By Darlene M. O'Sullivan

 Mary's humanity and her total trust in God's direction of her life can be understood with meditation on the Rosary. With the Annunciation – Angel Gabriel delivers the request of God the Father – "Would you be the Mother of My Son, by the aid of the Holy Spirit?" In her fiat, agreeing to be the God-bearer, she demonstrated total submission and obedience to God and established her relationship to the Trinity. Mary provides us not only with an example of how to live our lives but also a pathway through her to Christ. She lives for and with her Son, Jesus, and as mother for us.

 With the Incarnation of our Creator, taking on human flesh and our nature, God becomes one with us, showing us love and redeeming us. Mary, the creature, becomes the vehicle accomplishing this task. Christ is born of a woman in the same way all humanity enters this earthly life.

 Mary acknowledges the greatness of God and her lowliness in the <u>Magnificat</u> spoken to her cousin, Elizabeth, at the time of the Visitation (Luke: Chapter 1, verses 46-55).

 And Mary said:

> "My soul proclaims the greatness of the
> Lord;
> my spirit rejoices in God my Savior.

> For he has looked upon his handmaid's lowliness;
> behold, from now on all ages will call
> me blessed.
>
> The Mighty One has done great things for me,
> and holy is his name.
>
> His mercy is from age to age
> to those who fear him.
>
> He has shown might with his arm,
> dispersed the arrogant of mind and heart.
>
> He has thrown down the rulers from their thrones
> but lifted up the lowly.
>
> The hungry he has filled with good things;
> the rich he has sent away empty.
>
> He has helped Israel his servant,
> remembering his mercy.
>
> According to his promise to our fathers,
> to Abraham and to his descendents
> forever."

Remarkably in her situation, pregnant and not married, she transcended her human predicament and turned herself over to God's purpose for her life with faith and obedience.

Mary always reminds us of the mission her Son had in coming to dwell among us. The awareness of Christ's saving actions moves us to gratitude and adoration for His gift. In this way, we can truly honor Mary. Much the same way the Israelites were prone to honor biblical heroes i.e.: Moses parting the Red Sea [Exodus, Chapter 14], David defeating Goliath [1Samuel: Chapter 17, verses 41-51], and Gideon defeating the Midians with 300 soldiers giving honor to God who made these miracles possible. [Judges: 6:33-40; 7:1-22]

All of her apparitions carry the same message -- she is our mother and through her, Jesus is brought to us. By imitating her obedience to the Father, her devotion to her Son, and her cooperation with the Holy Spirit we can live for and with Christ.

Appendix IV

Consecration to Mary Immaculate
By Saint Maximilian Kolbe

O Immaculata, Queen of Heaven and Earth, refuge of sinners and are most loving Mother, God has willed to entrust the entire order of mercy to Thee.

I, _____ a repentant sinner, cast myself at Thy feet humbly imploring Thee to take me with all that I am and have, wholly to Thyself as Thy possession and property. Please make of me, of all my powers of soul and body, of my whole life, death and eternity, whatever most pleases Thee.

If it pleases Thee, use all that I am and have without reserve, wholly to accomplish what was said of Thee: "She will crush your head." And, "Thou alone have destroyed all heresies in the whole world."

Let me be a fit instrument in Thine Immaculate and merciful hands for introducing and increasing your glory to the maximum in all the many strayed and indifferent souls, and thus help extend as far as possible the blessed Kingdom of the Most Sacred Heart of Jesus. For wherever Thou enters, one obtains the grace of conversion and growth in holiness, since it is through Thy hands that all graces come to us from the most Sacred Heart of Jesus.

Date of my Consecration   Signature

Appendix V

Prayers of the Rosary

(**Bold** words indicate the leader's part when a group is praying.)

Apostles Creed

I believe in God the Father Almighty, Creator of heaven and earth; and in Jesus Christ, His only Son, our Lord, Who was conceived by the Holy Spirit, born of the Virgin Mary, suffered under Pontius Pilate, was crucified, died and was buried. He descended into hell; the third day He rose again from the dead. He ascended into heaven, and is seated at the right hand of God, the Father Almighty; from thence He shall come to judge the living and the dead. I believe in the Holy Spirit, the holy catholic church, the communion of saints, the forgiveness of sins, the resurrection of the body, and life everlasting. Amen.

Our Father

Our Father, who art in heaven, hallowed be Thy name; Thy kingdom come; Thy will be done on earth as it is in heaven. Give us this day our daily bread; and forgive us our trespasses, as we forgive those who trespass against us; and lead us not into temptation, but deliver us from evil. Amen.

Hail Mary

Hail Mary, full of grace, the Lord is with thee. Blessed art thou among women, and blessed is the fruit of thy womb, Jesus. Holy Mary, Mother of God, pray for us sinners, now and at the hour of our death. Amen.

Glory Be

***All* Glory be to the Father, and to the Son, and to the Holy Spirit;** as it was in the beginning, is now, and ever shall be, world without end. Amen.

*As stated on page 33 author adds the "all" when he prays the **Glory Be.***

Fatima Prayer

Oh my Jesus, forgive us our sins, save us from the fires of hell, lead all souls in to heaven, especially those in most need of Thy mercy.

Author says adds the following 2 Prayers
(Described on page 37)

My Jesus, we believe in You, we adore You, we trust in You, we love You. We beg pardon for those who do not believe in You, do not adore You, do not trust You and do not love You. (Requested by Mary.)
My Jesus please protect and save the unborn. (Due to the great number of abortions)

(These last 2 prayers are just said at the end of the Rosary)

Hail Holy Queen

Hail, Holy Queen, Mother of mercy, our life, our sweetness, and our hope! To Thee do we cry, poor banished children of Eve. To Thee do we send up our sighs mourning and weeping in this valley of tears. Turn then, Most Gracious Advocate, Thine eyes of mercy towards us, and after this our exile, show unto us the Blessed Fruit of Thy womb, Jesus. O clement, O loving, O sweet Virgin Mary. **Pray for us, O Holy Mother of God.** That we may be made worthy of the promises of Christ.

Prayer

O God! Whose only-begotten Son, by His life, death, and resurrection, has purchased for us the reward of eternal life; grant, we beseech Thee, that, meditating upon these mysteries of the Most Holy Rosary of the Blessed Virgin Mary, we may imitate what they contain and obtain what they promise. Through the same Christ our Lord. Amen.

May the divine assistance remain always with us. Amen. And may the souls of the faithful departed, through the mercy of God, rest in peace. Amen.

Holy Virgin, with thy loving Child, thy blessing give to us this day (or night).

In the name of the Father, and of the Son, and the Holy Spirit. Amen

Appendix VI

Prayer to Our Lady of the Miraculous Medal

Virgin Mother of God, Mary Immaculate, we unite ourselves to you under your title of our Lady of the Miraculous Medal. May this Medal be for each one of us a sure sign of your motherly affection for us and a constant reminder of our filial duties toward you. While wearing it, may we be blessed by your loving protection and preserved in the grace of your Son. Most powerful Virgin, Mother of our Savior, keep us close to you every moment of our lives so that like you we may live and act according to the teaching and example of your Son. Obtain for us, your children, the grace of a happy death so that in union with you we may enjoy the happiness of heaven forever. Amen.

Biblical Reference

Saint Joseph Giant Type Edition of the New American Bible: Translated from the Original Languages with Critical Use of All the Ancient Sources: Including the Revised New testament and the Revised Psalms. New York: Catholic Book Pub., 1992.

Contact the Author

Do you want to contact Bernie?

His email is gracesandluv@gmail.com.